10 Secrets You Need To Know About Men

Dating Coach Tells All!

By Gregg Michaelsen

10 Secrets You Need to Know About Men
A Dating Coach Tells All!

ISBN: 978-1-5481-4119-6

DISCLAIMER: As a male dating coach I am very good at what I do because of my years of studying the nuances of interpersonal relationships. I have helped thousands of women understand men. That said, I am not a psychologist, doctor or licensed professional. So do not use my advice as a substitute if you need professional help.

CONTENTS

Introduction:
The 10 Secrets You Need To Know About Men 5

CHAPTER 1: The Conveyor Belt to Manhood 9

CHAPTER 2: Let's Solve Guy Problems by Using His DNA . 17

CHAPTER 3: Man Mode Cheat Sheet:
        The 2 Key Concepts 29

CHAPTER 4: The 10 Secrets 33

CHAPTER 5: A Real Life Example Showing
        How Change Can Save a Marriage 65

Final Thoughts 69

Author Bio 71

Get The Word Out To Your Friends! 74

INTRODUCTION

The 10 Secrets You Need To Know About Men

Are you pissed off that life didn't give you an instruction manual to understand men? I would be!

In this book you will discover the 10 secrets to get whatever you want from a man simply by changing the way you communicate with him to terms that he understands. I call this Man Mode and it's a game changer!

> Women over-complicate the male mind!
> Uncomplicate it with this FREE infographic-
> **www.whoholdsthecardsnow.com/10-secrets-sign/**

I did it! I cracked the code and I did it with your help! Your thousands of emails resulting from 250,000 sales of my best-selling books sent me into the trenches on Saturday nights to interview and understand men.

Is this another short term way to manipulate men?

Playing games to manipulate men does not last, but communicating with him like his best male buddy can. Now that's a win/win for both of you. He will never know what hit him or why he wants to commit to you and only you.

You see, once you understand what makes up a man's DNA (and accept it) you can take any situation and just plug it into my model below. Just pick the DNA that applies to him in the given situation, go into Man Mode, and **Snap**, you just solved your problem!

No more philosophical crap from magazines and gurus that spew crap and confuse you even more.

I give you **tons** of examples that you can both relate to and fix with Man Mode. I also give you true stories of how I solved actual clients' problems by executing the strategies listed below.

We learn to fix:

- A guy spending too much time with his friends

- Sex, when it has all but dried up

- A man who won't do his chores around the house

- Laziness

- Men who pull away and how you can pull him back (video with Helen Fisher and me!)

- Being single by attracting a Lion through challenge and mystery

- Guys who won't show their emotions

- And **everything** else!

Oh, and remember the 400, 4 ½ star reviews from *To Date a Man You Must Understand a Man*? That book only touches on what we are about to discover below!

So enough with the pitch.

In this book we start with understanding the male mind and why we are the way we are based on the DNA instilled in us growing up. I call this, *The Conveyer Belt to Manhood*. At the end of this amazing chapter you might have to sit down and catch your breath! It's okay; thousands of women have thought the same thing, and just as many have asked where this information was years ago?

Next, for those that accept my mind-altering conclusions, I show you exactly how you can apply this knowledge towards men so you can acquire what you want from us. I then take it out of philosophical terms and give you 6 real-life examples. Again, you may want to sit down before you read this chapter.

Then, I explain the 10 secrets that help hammer down my points.

And finally, I prove my results with true coaching stories.

CHAPTER 1

The Conveyor Belt to Manhood

This chapter comes out of my #1 best seller *To Date a Man You Must Understand a Man*. I am updating and repeating it right here because it is so important.

It makes me nauseous to talk about hunting and gathering but, I'm sorry, men need to acquire things, very important things, if we are to be **true men**. We are taught that winning is everything, and to have a great career is a must. We are told we must be able to afford expensive material items like clothes and sports cars. And yes, we are taught to sleep with a lot of women.

Am I proud of this? No, but let me continue.

Society plucks us (men) from the womb and places us on the conveyer belt to manhood.

Think of a man as a chocolate chip cookie getting cranked out at the Keebler Chips Ahoy factory. Let's start with the ingredients: competition, challenge, status, self-worth, toughness, and motivation to make money and provide. All of this gets mixed into the batter and thrown into the 375 degree oven. A man is being created!

Hot out of the oven, our parents paint our room blue and stencil tough animals on the wall. Dad starts playing rough with us and challenges us to do better, win, and **never** cry.

Before we realize it, we are climbing trees, learning to fight, strapped into skis, and taught to be tough. Soon, we are washing the car, bringing in the groceries, cutting the lawn, and fixing the leaky sink. At fourteen, I was working at a local farm ripping out weeds surrounding tomato plants for rubles an hour.

For the first time, even though I was making hardly any money and felt part of forced child labor, I had a sense of self-worth and freedom. Yes, I had an allowance, but that was given to me. I didn't want things to be given to me. Well, I did, but I got more satisfaction with the pittance I got from pulling weeds. I earned that money.

I was no longer told what to do with my money by my parents. It was my money to blow on popsicles and bicycle parts.

It became increasingly evident that my manhood was defined by what I did, how well I did it, and how I compared to my peers. Like a monarch butterfly emerging from a chrysalis, status was becoming the cornerstone of my universe. With status came confidence and with confidence came a man who could begin to understand the world, provide, and love.

Money became important.

Today, I see relationships fall apart because a man has no self-worth or confidence. He has lost his way and is not living up to what he should be. Some men fall off the **conveyer belt** early, and are placed in the "reject" pile. This usually has a lot to do with their inability to provide. They can't get a job or their jobs are very low paying and/or bring no status.

I know this sounds shallow, but it's how men are internally wired. Men turn to drugs and alcohol when they feel they don't measure up to their peers or to their parents' expectations. They emotionally (and sometimes physically) abuse people, or they feel the need to sleep with as many women as possible to try to prove their self-worth. Of course, ultimately, this is a no-win and a very toxic endeavor.

Other rejects (or **wet kittens,** as I call them) are men who never had a fighting chance. They grew up without a dad or older brother, or with parents who were drug addicts or alcoholics. Maybe they couldn't get out of the hood and were forced to join gangs.

Of course, this leads to a path of sadness, loneliness, and depression.

And guess what? Many women pick these types of men and don't even know it! Or they do know it and they think that they can fix them – they **can't!**

Men are providers. It is in our DNA. Money is more important to men than most women realize. If a man can't pay the rent, afford a car, or afford to put food on the table, how can he ever measure up to himself and to you?

He can't.

A man must complete his mission to manhood by becoming self-reliant. This is defined by who he is, how much he makes, and how he is defined by the important people in his life.

Until he becomes self-reliant, women will not and should not be a focus in his life.

But they are.

He might say he loves you and he wants to marry you some day, but in his mind you are dispensable until he has a better grasp on the definition and proof of the man he is. He might not even be aware of this. Men are providers who are responsible for the people they love and for their future offspring. If men can't provide, they feel like failures.

I am bombarded everyday with emails like this:

"Gregg, Jim and I have been together for 4 years. I supported him through most of this time. I was there for him while he went back to school. I gave it my all. Finally, he landed a great job, and about this time he said he doesn't love me anymore. I am heartbroken, this is my future man. Please help!"

See how this affects you? Until a man has self-worth, you are secondary. I'm sorry this is the case, but until you understand this, you will fail if you continue to choose these types of men.

You have the choice to stop right here, digest what I just told you and never pick a man like this ever again and change your life for the better!

Many women love their man unconditionally and can't understand why he won't reciprocate. "Sex is great and my Mom loves him," they say.

Money is not as important (I'm ruling out gold diggers) to most women as it is to men. Most women live a life of scarcity when it comes to their choices of guys to date, so when a wet kitten (that has some attractive traits) of a man arrives at their door they invite him in and dry off his fur. They figure that if they have money, then what's the problem?

I'll tell you what the problem is! He is a wet kitten! Women try to mold this man into greatness. They don't understand this is impossible for any length of time. This wet kitten needs to go back outside and grow into a **Lion.** You cannot do this for him. Instead, you let him inside to pee on the rug for months or even years, and before you know it, you could find yourself forty-two years old, heartbroken, and single.

Know that this is not your fault! You simply don't understand men, and this book is going to change that!

Of course, there are exceptions to everything. If a twenty-year-old man is on his way to completing his engineering degree or a guy is nearing the end of a vocational school course to be a car mechanic, he knows his realization to provide is close to fruition. These men might be ready to love a woman.

You need to choose men, choose wisely, and not be chosen. There are millions of wet kittens out there but there are millions of full grown Lions out there too. In order to experience lasting love you need to pick from the full-grown lion bin!

There is one catch, though: the full-grown lions don't patronize the usual watering holes. Very few **Mufasas** are bar flies hanging out on a Saturday night. They don't need to chase women.

They attract women where ever they go!

Lions are choosers, too. They want interesting, motivated, high-value women. Women with integrity and boundaries, women who know what they want in life and in a man.

I will help make you this woman!

Some things to remember:

- Understand the influences society puts on men

- Understand the ingredients or DNA that make-up a man — including competition, challenge, self-worth, toughness, and motivation to make money and provide

- Money brings men status and is very important to all men, even though it is not necessarily important to you

- How a man is viewed by others, mainly by male role models, correlates directly to his self-esteem

- Men are not able to love themselves, or women, until they have attained what they consider to be success

- Women tend to date wet kittens because they feel they can change them. You can't! Wet kittens pee on the rug, ultimately leave, and never come back

- Lions don't hang out at the usual watering holes — they are choosers, too

CHAPTER 2

Let's Solve Guy Problems by Using His DNA

This is a very exciting chapter. DNA is a bitch!

So now you know what goes into our DNA. You have discovered our DNA bag of goodies, if you will. Now you know that competition is important to us, winning is a must, money is our status symbol, and status, as it compares to our peers, is very important.

You now understand that we withdraw our emotions because we were taught to do so as kids when we were not winning, not providing, or not being appreciated. You understand (but do not like) that we ogle at women because we were taught to sleep with as many as possible. You understand that we like when you show us appreciation. These attributes stay with men, in varying amounts, even as we get older.

Again, I am not always proud of how I am but these are the facts. Also remember that these characteristics are not just my personal perspective — these truths have been gathered over years, by me, through thousands of one-on-one interviews with men.

Let's review the ingredients that go into men:

1) We need to win; winning is everything!

2) Competition is huge

3) We fear rejection

4) We hold in our emotions

5) Money is very important to us

6) Status and how we measure up to our peers rank high

7) We love challenge, and we need it to win

8) We need to feel appreciated

9) We were taught to sleep with as many women as we can

10) We need to feel that we can provide

11) We take longer to fall in love

12) We can get bored easy when the challenge and mystery disappear, so we frequently seek change

Every emotion we show and action we take can be tied directly to the 12 ingredients above which make up our DNA.

Knowing this, you can now determine where a man is, mentally, in life right down to the week, the day, or at a single moment in time. Then, you can take the necessary steps to "tweak his behavior" so you can get your man back on track if he is going rogue.

Can you imagine having this power to evaluate why we are acting the way we are at any moment? And then doing something about it to redirect us?!

WHOA!

You can. And with this power you will stop blaming yourself for how he is acting or reacting. Instead, you can act in a new way that a man will understand and capitulate so he see things your way. All this is done by simply understanding how the male mind works, and then changing how we react.

Below, I am going to show you everyday examples that you can use!

Example #1

The facts: I come home from work depressed because I did not get the raise.

The DNA is affected: My ability to provide has taken a hit. I lost today. I needed to win.

How you react: You want to talk and try to comfort me. You may try to fix the problem by offering to help pay for the mortgage. I get mad and short tempered. I feel emasculated. You take it personally. Then you try even harder, or you get angry. You start to feel under appreciated. Contempt builds.

The solution you are now learning: You understand what happened and you give me space. You understand that this has nothing to do with you so you go about your business and let me pout in my man cave. Then, as I recover slightly, you start to show some small appreciation for something I did well lately. Do this, and I will want to communicate soon.

Example #2

The facts: Leslie has a new boyfriend named Keith. She is spending more and more time at Keith's house. Slowly she is acquiring more drawers, at Keith's suggestion, in which to keep her stuff. Suddenly, Keith starts to realize that he has an exclusive girlfriend and starts to pull back.

The DNA is affected: Keith, although suggesting Leslie take as much space as she wants, is starting to feel squeezed and pressured. His friends ask him out on Saturday night and he realizes that there will be consequences if he goes. Keith is not in love yet, but Leslie is well on her way. Remember #11 from above? Guys take longer to fall in love.

Leslie's reaction: Leslie did the natural thing, right? She was over four to five nights a week so it made sense to not pack so much stuff. She was treating "moving her stuff in" as a milestone in their relationship. I get that. But guys don't understand what a "milestone" is; Keith was just having fun and living in the moment. He didn't realize that (I know, we are stupid) Leslie was starting to fall in love and therefore spending less time with her friends and all her free time with Keith. Keith felt like Leslie was "making him her hobby" so he started to withdraw.

The solution you are now learning: Leslie should have **never** moved her stuff into Keith's apartment, even though Keith suggested it. She should have said some high-value comment like "When I feel you are the man for me, then I will consider a drawer!" And she would have said it with a smile. Also, she should have never given up her friends and her hobbies to be with Keith. This would have impressed Keith and made him try harder! He would have felt challenged, and would have quickly realized that he was not Leslie's main attraction, at least not yet.

Example #3
The facts: Kim was paying for dates because her boyfriend Jeff could not afford to. She also did his laundry and encouraged him to fill out job applications.

The DNA is affected: Almost everything in Jeff's DNA bag was declining, in his mind. He had no job, so he had no money or status. He was not appreciated. He was being taken care of by a woman who was not his mom – the exact job that *he* was built for.

How you react: Kim did everything for Jeff. She thought that she could motivate Jeff by taking care of him and that when she did, everything would be great. Instead, their sex life fell apart and Jeff was turning into a couch potato, drinking often, and demonstrating no motivation.

The opposite was happening. Jeff felt like a loser around Kim. She had turned into his mother and no guy likes that. He was emasculated. He cheated on Kim and they broke up. He got a job and found a new girlfriend that he proudly posted all over FB.

Kim was devastated. She blamed herself, and this experience ripped another slice of confidence out of her. Why? Because she did not understand the male mind and how to deal with her guy.

Again, let's explore.

The solution you are now learning: Kim should have backed off and let Jeff solve his problems without getting involved. She should have been supportive from a distance. She should have run to her friends and stuck to her passions. Kim would have been better served by setting a date limit in case Jeff could not fix his issues within a reasonable time. Then, had he not solved his issues, she should have moved on and dated others. Jeff ultimately did solve his problems but Kim missed out because she did not understand the male mind.

Example #4

The facts: Jim cuts the front lawn and stops for a beak. Jenny, his wife, is pissed because the kids are having a tent stay over and he did not finish mowing the back lawn. Jenny yells at Jim and Jim withdrawals to his garage to work on his Mustang GT.

The DNA is affected: Recall #8 above: We need to feel appreciated. Jim got nothing out of cutting the front lawn. He got yelled at, so why should he cut the back lawn (which he was planning on doing) and get yelled at again? He won't, and contempt will build and drip by drip these two will be heading to divorce court.

The solution you are now learning: Jenny should have taken a better tact, like saying, according to my rules, "Jim! Hey, awesome job, my dear, the lawn looks great and you even missed my Lilies – thanks! Can you do the back lawn for the kids' sleep over? I will make the lemonade ☺"

It is important to look at the ingredients that make up his DNA because there lies the answer. In this case, Jenny's solution (had she known) was to show her man **appreciation**.

If Jim was rewarded with appreciation, he would have been happy. He would have won. He would have known he did well and would have wanted to keep it going and get even more appreciation from his wife. He would have cut the backyard, and the side yard to boot. Hell, he may have even cut the neighbor's lawn!

Gregg, this cannot be this simple!

Oh yeah? Then try it and see if you can prove me wrong! I can give you a solution to any guy problem simply by looking into a man's bag of DNA and having you react accordingly!

Let's keep going.

Example #5

The facts: Monica has been trying to get Gilles (her husband) to paint the extra bedroom for the last four months. Gilles keeps saying he will, but he always makes an excuse.

The DNA is affected: Painting the extra room doesn't trigger winning, or challenge, or any of the main DNA ingredients and so Gilles has no real motivation.

Monica's reaction: This makes Monica angry and she starts coming unglued about how lazy he is.

The solution you are now learning: Instead of getting angry at Gilles, Monica calmly says to Gilles, "Honey, don't worry about painting the room; I called Paradise Painting and they will come paint this weekend."

Now Gilles's senses are aroused. He doesn't want another guy, a strange guy who he has to pay no less, walking into his house and doing his job! No way. **Challenge** has been brought into the equation, something he knows all about, and he will rise to the occasion and paint the room. The room is baby blue with an off-white trim the next day!

Again, simply look to the ingredients that make up his DNA because there lies the answer. In this case her answer (had she known) was #7: we love challenge, and we need it to win.

Example #6

The facts: Debbie is in a failing marriage. She is losing Jim to his friends and the sex is gone.

The DNA is affected: **Men love challenge** and **men get bored easily.** Jim hasn't won at anything lately. He forgot what a challenge was.

The solution: She contacted me and we changed her entire routine! See below for the full story.

Jim gets home every night at seven and expects Debbie to have dinner on the table—she is a great cook. Jim has been going out with his friends more and more and Debbie thinks that he might be having, or soon will have, an affair. She emailed me for advice.

The next night, Jim came home at seven and Debbie was gone. Jim was upset, as you might expect. He called her and texted her over and over. Debbie answered after a few texts and said that she was out with her friends (she lied; she was with her Mom). She told Jim that she had left dinner in the fridge and that he could heat it up himself. He was dumb-founded. He started "anger texting" and Debbie calmly replied, "Sorry babe, I want to see my friends."

Notice, she didn't start a fight or go into this long rant about how he is able to see his friends and she never can, blah, blah blah. Debbie just changed her routine and did something for herself.

In the coming weeks, Debbie reestablished relationships with some old friends and found some new hobbies. She rediscovered her passion for hiking, too. Fortunately, she has a decent job which means she has the financial means to do her own thing. She mixed things up by changing her routine and she did this, literally, in two weeks!

Jim? Jim stopped seeing his friends and started concentrating on his (as Debbie claims) "new wife," Debbie! You see, it wasn't fun anymore going to see his friends when he knew that his wife was out with "her friends." He now takes Debbie out to dinner and Debbie cooks when she is in the mood. And speaking of "in the mood," Jim started getting in the mood for sex again. Of course, Debbie now controls that, too.

Long story short, Debbie changed up her routine and concentrated on herself; that's all.

Is this a game? I don't think so, but you can call it what you want. I just call it a touchdown on Debbie's part. The game is when I mentor women with this stuff and they fake it. They pretend to be working on themselves when they are not, and guys see right through this.

Yes, Debbie lied about where she was the first night because she had to, but she quickly corrected that by hanging out with real friends and pursuing real hobbies of her own. She changed "her story," and she did it at 43 years old! Debbie understood what Jim was going through, and simply responded with the right course of action.

The Take-Away

Men seek routine, and then they get bored. Women provide this environment without knowing it. Break your routine and be unavailable once in a while, and watch the magic happen. The instant that Jim started to wonder where Debbie was and who she was with, (when she should be, in his eyes, sticking to "the routine" and staying home), he got confused and Debbie piqued his interest again. **Challenge** and **mystery** were created and their relationship regained its balance.

Game. Set. Match!

Looking at all these examples above, they probably appear quite small and insignificant to you. In fact, individually, they are. But when you string together three or four of these examples per day, they become very powerful and help a man feel good about himself and his relationship.

Now, instead of a man getting hit with three or four toxic salvos that hurt him and build contempt, he is now racking up more and more positive experiences and he is falling more and more in love!

How? You have simply started understanding men (and accepted how we are) and are now able to communicate your needs to them in terms that he responds to positively, all while you got what you want. Talk about a win/win!

One caveat; make sure that you are dating a worthy man — a LION. If a man is too far gone because of some traumatic past event or he is addicted to drugs, porn, or alcohol, then do not bother unless he has fixed, or is fixing, these issues! You can't get a broken man to love you who will not first fix his own issues.

For those of you asking why you should always be the one to change for a man, please understand that I am subsequently teaching men how to be more understanding of women. This is a two way street.

CHAPTER 3

Man Mode Cheat Sheet: The 2 Key Concepts

So now that you are understanding men better and have some great examples on how to deal with us, based on our 12 DNA imprints, let's continue. These next two "act like a guy" concepts will help you in many of the situations that you will encounter. Pick one and apply it.

Act like a guy

- Treat him like his best male friend treats him

- Act like he acts towards you, but do it first

Treat him like his best friend treats him

Many women get jealous of their man's best friend's relationship. I don't blame you. Heck, they always want to be together, they share everything — things you don't get to hear, and they even touch and (almost) cry together. They have silly handshakes and they speak their own child-like language, right?

So wouldn't it make sense that this might work for you, too? It will!

By treating your guy, on occasion, like his best friend treats him, you will "train" him into treating you better.

Here are some examples:

Texting: Guys text in short sentences and without emotion. They don't check in and see how they are doing all day. Try it. You will find that he will text more because he will wonder what you are doing.

Be direct: Guys tell each other that their shirt sucks, or their hair looks like crap. Try it. Just make sure you say it with a laugh and in a bit more subtle manner so you don't come across as being mean.

Challenge him: This is a huge one. Guys challenge each other 24/7 and they love it. This is how they communicate. Try it. Beat him to the coffee shop. Kick his butt at chess. It doesn't matter if you win or lose — just challenge him!

Act childish: It's okay to act like a little kid now and then! Guys do it all the time when they are together. Stupid handshakes, making faces at each other, doing impressions of some guy — it's all good. Try it!

By treating him like his best friend does, you are communicating in his language, a language that is never threatening to him and is always inviting. I have seen women steal their man back from their guy friends by simply using this behavior.

Act like he acts towards you, but do it first

This is touched on in secret #9 but I will expand upon it here. Again, this works for him so will it work for you? **Yes!**

It works because it gets his attention on so many levels. It shakes his "DNA tree" like a strong gust of wind!

For example, 30 minutes before the super bowl, prior to him heading to his best friend's party (that you were never *really* invited to), leave before him to go to your own party! Go happily, and wish him fun.

This leaves his brain scattered, wondering why he wasn't invited and wondering who is going to be there. Mystery kicks in, the challenge to try harder surfaces, and freedom is granted to him. **Whoa!** You just proved how high-value you really are. Needless to say, you will be invited to the next party.

Summarizing the Man Mode Cheat Sheet

The cheat sheet works when you need help navigating his behavior. "How does *Man Mode* apply in this situation? What would Gregg suggest?" Simply think in terms of acting like he would, or acting like his best friend would, and **pow** you have your answer.

Remember, don't abuse this power and don't make what you are doing obvious. The pure subtlety of the strategy makes it incredibly influential.

> If this amazes you, as it should, then I have something you will LOVE. It's a mastery class of these skills called
> *The Man Whisperer Program.*
> (www.whoholdsthecardsnow.com/product/the-man-whisperer/)

CHAPTER 4
The 10 Secrets

SECRET #1: Winning is Everything to Men

Talking to my middle aged readers and talking on Saturday nights with college women, I get asked the same questions about dating and relationships. My answer is like a taped message ... **you gals don't understand men!**

That's the short answer. The long answer goes like this:

Everything we do is centered on winning!

It's #1 on your list above, but it may not stand out like it should. We are taught not to cry because crying is done by the losing side. Challenge? That's involved in the process of winning. We don't just want to beat the easy opponent; we want to come out ahead of all the alpha males, too. Boredom? That comes from having nothing more to win or no competition in the foreseeable future. Money? Money beats the competition. I can drive a nicer car and live in a nicer home than my neighbor because of the all-mighty dollar. Rejection? Rejection is the result of losing, and so it is feared by men. I can go on and on how **winning** is an obsession.

And yet when I explain how important winning is, women look at me cross-eyed. "What the heck are you talking about?"

This stuff will never be found online or in magazines. They **all** miss this!

But it all makes sense and fits perfectly into the "man puzzle" when you think about it.

- Guys will shut down in the middle of a relationship because they lost their job or they did not get the raise.

- A guy who recently got dumped will not put his everything into you if you are his new girl.

- A woman emasculates her man and then she wonders why he stopped calling her.

- Fido, his best friend second to you, croaks and he withdraws.

- His NFL team just lost the super bowl.

Why do men react this way?

These men lost!

If a man did not get the loan he needed to expand his business — he lost. If he is bored with no win in sight because he has won everything, he may feel like he lost. Billionaires want to be presidents. Why? They need to win. Sound familiar Mr. Trump?

A man will prioritize winning over their relationship in most cases. This does not mean that he does not love you; no, it means that something in his life is "in a losing stage" and he needs some time to deal with it. Women take this personally when they shouldn't. Instead, they should let him withdraw and get on with their other priorities. This, in turn, will actually make him feel like a winner in the relationship when he does get over, or conquers, his loss.

To further complicate things, women don't need this **winning** trait to be happy. Men ask. *"Am I winning?"* Women ask, *"Am I being loved?"*

Men feel enormous pressure to succeed. That is our goal. Many men cannot hit that mark and will distract themselves with useless pursuits that keep them from their mission of winning and succeeding. Women, not having the least understanding of this, will take these types of man in (wet kittens) and try to fix them. It never works.

I always like to use the example of the spoiled rich kid who inherited his daddy's money. This guy almost always has problems, because the winning step was left out. He never achieved anything, and yet he ended up with the winning results. He will eventually fail in life.

"OK, Gregg, I believe this but what do I do?"

First, you pick a guy who is driven. Pick a motivated man. This guy is "in the game" and putting himself out there. He is studying for something or he has a good job that keeps him positive about the future. Pick a man who has hobbies and friends. Look for a guy who has failed and then bounced back with a vengeance. Winners fail all the time because they know they must do so in order to succeed. They fall and get back up.

Avoid the wet kittens – the guys still living with mom, over-drinking and using drugs, and the guys bouncing from crappy job to crappy job while you pay for everything!

After picking a **Lion**, make him **feel** like a winner. A woman should support a man (not try to fix him) on his quest, believe in him, and fully understand that she might be secondary on certain days while he is fulfilling his mission. This type of reaction will win him over and make you feel loved. Whereas a woman who whines and yells at her man for not making her number one all the time will lose him.

When he does have his losing days, give him space, and focus on your girlfriends and hobbies. Realize that this has nothing to do with you and his love for you. Let him reach out when he is ready and go right back into your supportive role.

Six years ago, I was writing and helping guys (and women) with their dating issues. I talked about publishing and becoming a dating and life coach fulltime but I did not (totally) believe in myself. My girlfriend did! She said, "Do it." She didn't do it for me, but she believed in me more than I believed in myself. She motivated me to take the next step.

And you know what happened? I fell madly in love with this woman because she supported and spoke to me in my "male love language" that I could connect with. She helped me **win by believing in me!**

See the difference between how most women react and how women should react? It's very simple and yet so powerful!

Do this and watch the magic happen!

In Summary
Read over this chapter and thank your lucky stars someone wrote it! Hahaha. Are you starting to realize that we are not as complicated as you thought we are? We are just different – horses of a different color. Women want to feel loved and men need to win! Don't fight it, just understand and then take the necessary (and easy) actions above. We are not changing you, we are just changing your reactions to us.

SECRET #2: Rejection Hurts!
This makes sense because rejection is the result of losing, but few women **really** realize how much rejection hurts us. Especially when it comes from women. Rejection from a woman is like a double blow because we are taught to provide for women; when the very subject we are built to provide for rejects us the loss is compounded.

I realize this fear when working with men. In fact, many men will pass on trying to win over a woman because of their fear of rejection. This can be seen on any given night at a social venue. Only the winners will approach. Of course, many of these winners are also players. The less confident men sit on their butts and talk to their friends to avoid any chance of rejection.

Women may not realize the magnitude of rejection that men feel. We are not as tough as you think. We are vulnerable. We are vulnerable and we cannot express it to our peers because we don't share our emotions like you do, therefore we have no outlet. It's like some sort of cruel joke. This builds up and we are soon curled up in a ball in our living room opting out of dating all together. We become non-committal men.

Women are taught that it's up to the man to approach, but they do all the wrong things to encourage it. Women barely look over, and rarely smile at men. Their body language screams, "Get lost creep!" Women also tend to huddle together like a lion pride ready to kill.

We will approach if we know that our odds are good. The problem is that we need a whack in the head to realize that you are interested. Give us that whack in the head! Smile, walk by us, poke us in the ass with the end of that umbrella thing in your drink!

In my best seller, *The Social Tigress*, chapter four is called "So This Girl Walks into a Bar." This chapter is spectacular and will teach you the necessary body language that will help a man believe his odds are good with meeting you, and therefor minimize his rejection fears.

Rejection rears its ugly head in relationships, too. Telling us we are performing poorly in the bedroom, putting us down in front of others, and shooting down our ideas are toxic to us – it slowly kills us.

Even trying to change us is a form of rejection. Many women think that getting married will motivate him to get a better job and stop partying so much. Why will he? This says that you don't like the way he is and you want him to change or, even worse, that you can fix him.

So what's a woman to do?

This does not mean that you should become a yes woman to everything he does. Just be aware of the crushing affect that rejection has on a man, especially in the bedroom. Know that when he withdraws, you have pushed too hard. Read his body language to understand his limits. Help show him where you differ and lead with a compliment. "Babe that feels great, now go a bit lower," is much better than, "Will you ever get this right?!" Basically, be more patient and add a touch of admiration.

See the difference?

Again, we are not seeking to change you; we are enabling you to understand your man and making slight but **powerful** changes to how you interact with him. Patience, leading with a compliment, and reading his body language can cure a mountain of contempt versus an immediate put down, rolling of your eyes, or an insult.

Tweak your reactions and his fear of rejection can be all but eliminated!

SECRET #3: Guys Go After What They Want

How many times have you asked yourself, or me, if a guy likes you? You ask yourself, "Why doesn't he ask me out?" "Am I just a friend?" "Is he too shy?" "Does he think that I am too good for him?" Yes, this last question gets asked, too.

A woman will then look for any and every sign that points to yes. She will be convinced that the man is into her and ignore any signs that he is not. She will create her own narrative because she is like a horse with blinders. In fact, she might even think that she will be rewarded, somehow, if she continues to think this way.

I own a construction company. We set ceramic tile, stone, and glass. Customers will look at four pieces of tile shown on a sample board at the tile store. They love these four pieces. Then, they get it home and they see 1000 pieces installed on their floor all grouted and they hate it.

When you think you are attracted to a man you need to see all the pieces, not just the pieces that you want to look at.

True story: I went out with a girl friend of mine in Boca. She wanted to get my take on this guy she "loved" and was convinced was into her. She said he was shy and she wanted me to be the conduit to get him to ask her out. We were with a group of her girlfriends and this guy opened up to one of her girlfriend's big time! Oh he was into her alright, it just wasn't *her* that he was into – it was her attractive friend.

This guy was not only not shy, he was cocky and he went right after the girl he wanted. This is how guys are!

The funny thing? My friend still would not believe me because they had a "nice talk." **Really?**

Guys Go After What They Want
In my #1 best seller, *To Date a Man You Must Understand a Man*, I teach women that men go after what they want! They rarely hide it. I also teach women how we are simple creatures and women try to turn us into these complicated aliens – we are not!

So if a man likes you, he will make it obvious. We are simple; there is an "on" button, and there is an "off" button – that's it. He may not go after you in a very good way, but that's not my point; he will go after what he wants. In fact, everyone in the room will probably know what he wants except the woman that he doesn't want who wants him!

Look at His Actions; Don't Listen to His Words
It's simple. If he buys you a drink, he wants to get to know you. If he asks you out, and then follows up the next day, he likes you. If he helps you move your furniture, he likes you. If you meet his Mom and his kids, he really likes you. This means you have survived (and he has survived) round one. But there are more rounds.

On the other hand, if he talks about getting together, and he talks about you meeting his family, blah, blah, blah, but he never follows through, then he does **not** like you!

But I Can Change His Mind With Your Help Gregg, Right?

Ah, no.

Certain qualities trigger attraction in a man both physically and personality wise. He might like a tall woman and you are short. He might like a larger woman and you are muscular and thin. He might like a loud and giggly woman and you are shy and reserved.

You have your list too, right? You might want a man who doesn't have kids. Or is super funny. Are you going to be happy with a divorced guy with three kids who is serious? Probably not, so why try to make yourself like him? You shouldn't try.

My point is that you shouldn't try to make any guy like you if he does not show outward signs. Yes, make your move or give him the opportunity to ask you out, but if he does not, say goodbye. Don't take it personally and move on immediately without looking back – ever!

If you do not, another notch of self-esteem will be taken from you.

Instead, here is some life altering advice: build your own life without a man, love yourself, pursue every dream you ever had, and watch your self-assurance soar! Then watch as the men line up outside your confidence door!

So Why Do Guys Lead Women On?

Now, obviously, some men are just total assholes – you have dated a few, I'm sure.

But most guys don't mean to lead women on. They want to get to know a woman so they are aggressive at the beginning. Then, when they realize that she is not the one, they slowly back away. This is that dark and murky period when women usually contact me. There is a period when a guy needs to find the answer on his own and women often take this as "He is definitely into me!" when he is not, necessarily.

Then, the "What am I doing wrong?" questions pop up.

There are no mixed signals! He either likes you or not. If your intuition is confused, then he is not into you. Period. Move on!

So if you are getting the avoidance act, the texts are slowing, and the excuses are piling up, it's time to re-focus your energy back on you and other men.

SECRET #4: Release the Chains

Men want the feeling of freedom. Notice how I framed that statement. The *feeling of freedom* is not to say they don't want a relationship – most do, but they don't want to be discouraged from living their lives and pursuing their interests. Many men feel like women want to contain them and design their lives as they see fit. Often times women do not even realize they are doing this.

I recorded a video with world renowned Doctor Helen Fisher describing our fear of commitment. You can see it at: https://www.whoholdsthecardsnow.com/yourtango-the-experts-why-do-men-get-spooked/. I politely explain to the lady experts (to their horror) that we fear our money being taken away, being forced to distance ourselves from our friends, and finally, we fear never being able to have sex with another woman. Then I explain how these fears can be easily neutralized.

A man needs to recharge and sometimes it is done best by being with his friends. Let him go golfing or take a ski trip; you should do the same with your friends. To do this you need trust. To have trust, you each need confidence. I teach the cultivation and execution of both in my other books. Never make your guy your hobby. Keep your own, participate in his, and he should reciprocate by participating in yours. Also, find one hobby that you can participate in together. This "releases the chains" and gives him a feeling of freedom. He feels like he has won the battle that other couples can't seem to win.

I can't count how many friends I have (or used to have) who I never see because they are not allowed to grab a drink with me on a random Saturday night. Really? Are their wives/girlfriends convinced that we will all hit a strip club and pay women for sex? If this is their concern or if their guys will actually do this, then they have bigger problems.

So it goes without saying that many of these couples will break up and, in fact, some of mine already have.

A simpler example of giving a man his freedom is letting him withdraw to his garage to work on his car alone all day. No big deal, just let him. He has something on his mind. He needs to pull back. Bring him some lemonade, give him a big kiss, and go grab lunch with your girls! He will love you for it and you will see the reciprocation, I promise you!

Unfortunately, this rarely happens and it's easy to understand why. Women don't pull back when they are in love so why do we need to? She is upset, so she pursues her guy to settle her doubt of whether or not he is still in love with her. Then, when he stays withdrawn, she, more often than not, will rip him a new one because he didn't spend his afternoon with her.

Things domino. Her man then feels trapped and withdraws even more when he isn't able to escape and reset. He knows that if he does, his significant other will be upset.

This resetting does not always happen at the most convenient time either – this is life. Couples who learn to give each other this healthy and much needed time and space become more of a team – they become closer. I can't tell you how many times I was given my space and all I could think about was my girl! Try it and watch your phone light up with happy texts saying how much he misses you when it's only the first quarter of the Ohio State game ☺.

SECRET #5: Men Take Longer to Fall in Love

A while back I met a beautiful woman from Russia in Delray, FL. No, she was not a paid Russian bride or a spy, haha. We spent three wonderful days together, and then I had to leave and go back to my home in Boston. She was bummed. I asked her if she wanted to join me in Boston for the rest of her vacation. She said yes and we had a wonderful time.

I quickly realized that we were not on the same page.

I was getting to know her and having fun living in the moment. Unbeknownst to me, she was sizing me up to be a husband and father. Her decision, it seemed, was already made and I was naïve and just having fun with the discovery process. She perceived my invitation for her to join me in Boston to mean that I wanted her to be my wife, because that was **her** goal.

So what's the problem here?

Men don't fall in love like that. We take time. Svetlana was reading into our relationship differently than I was. I was getting to know her, while she had already determined our fate and anything that did not fit this narrative was a disappointment to her.

The irony? Because she was moving so fast, I never got to know her for fear of really letting her down! It was easier to just end things. Looking back, sadly, I really liked her but I will never know what might have been.

For more on this exact subject please watch another video with the pros and me at: https://www.whoholdsthecardsnow.com/yourtango-the-experts-is-there-love-at-first-sight/.

In this video you will see resistance from the women on the panel questioning my answer.

They are women – they can't possibly know how men feel!

In fact, after the shoot the male producer came up to me and quietly said, "You are so right, man!" Remember also, that my tactics have evolved over my 54 years and are the result of interviewing thousands of men. This is not just "Gregg" speaking.

You see, men live more in the moment than women do. We can't spot our next *relationship milestone* if it slapped us in the face. We are oblivious. Falling in love happens to us when it feels right. Women, on the other hand, seem to look at each positive event as a milestone to advance the relationship.

"I met his family"✓
"He took me away for the weekend"✓
"He said he loved me when he was drunk"✓
"His dog lapped my face – destiny!"✓

I did all these things with Svetlana, (my cat licked her face, no dog) but I was not anywhere near my milestone! She would have been better served to just roll with the weekend and let love happen – if it was going to happen at all. Women (in my opinion) need to live more in the moment, stay happy, and enjoy the process. There needs to be time for both parties to get to know each other before judgement, before the "all in" is declared, and men normally take longer.

That said, some men will take advantage of this time and drag out this period because they have some outside issues and are afraid of commitment. These men are wet kittens and should be avoided. That's why women should always set reasonable time limits.

SECRET #6: The Million Dollar Question, When Do Men Commit?

A man will commit when he realizes that he is more fulfilled with this woman in his life than he was when he was single and free.

Simple right? We don't think things through and we don't see milestones, we just suddenly realize the above statement is true and it happens! Unfortunately, as you can tell by my story above, women don't always allow this to happen because either they have a different deadline or they change because they think there is something they are doing wrong.

Guys will usually take longer to commit. Women, many of whom lack confidence and/or don't understand men, do **not** pick up on this fact and immediately think that something is wrong. This changes the entire dynamic that the man (and the woman) were enjoying. She is on a timeline and living in the future of perceived happiness together. He is just having fun and enjoying the relationship in the moment.

The relaxed situation now becomes jeopardized, just like it did with Svetlana and me. She changed because she felt the need to get me on board with her timeline. I changed because I was not comfortable, and so I ran. Sound familiar?

So timing is often a problem. To her credit, Svetlana was headed back to her country and she might have felt some desperation to advance the relationship because of the time and distance that were about to separate us from each other.

I once coached a young couple. Chris wanted to be financially stable before settling down, so he decided to delay his marriage. The timing was just not right for him. This was unacceptable to his fiancée, Connie. She thought he was just making excuses. After talking one on one with Chris, I knew he was being honest. The two of them made it clear that once Chris was out of school and landed his job (placement was guaranteed), that the marriage date would be set – this ultimately happened and Connie and Chris are doing very well today.

The Conveyer Belt to Manhood states that **being able to provide** is a priority over all things to a man, so Chris's timing took precedent.

Had Connie failed to come to an understanding of how the male mind works, this relationship might have failed. Connie might have put pressure on Chris and he might have capitulated. This could have created a whole lot of contempt within the marriage. Or, he would have simply broken up with her and stuck to his guns. Either way, neither of the two would be to blame, but **both** would have lost!

I hope that this example hits home and makes you realize just how important it is to understand the male mind.

I know, men need to understand women's minds, too – I am working on that!

We Are Not Tricking Men into Love

I have talked a lot about challenge and mystery and breaking routines in my books, but these behaviors are not meant to "trick" a man into loving you. Yes, they certainly will work short term and in the early stages of a relationship so that you are able to stand out from other women, but these traits are not about duping a man into love. Challenge and mystery are **fun to attain** and make you a better woman! In fact every high-value woman I know has a built in treasure chest oozing with challenge and mystery.

You can't make a man commit and love you, but you can make yourself a very lovable person! And a person who has a great story to tell is interesting and, therefore, lovable. An interesting person is naturally mysterious and has confidence as a result of all her experiences. This means she has opinions with which she can challenge others. Oh, and guess what? Guys just happen to love a woman who brings mystery and challenge to the table – it's part of our DNA.

So you see, I teach mystery and challenge not only because men are attracted to these two characteristics but also because women should be working on "their stories" long before they start to date.

Quality men (Lions) want to be in a relationship. They do not have commitment phobia. They just want an environment in which they are happier with a woman in their life (you) than they were when they were single and alone. It's just a matter of creating this environment. How does he feel when he is with you? Is he happy? Is he stressed out, or do you calm his stress when you are together?

Now that you have more clarity about the inner workings of our minds, you can create an environment in which he can retreat and where he can be happy! You can create a sanctuary from his stressful day and the place where his smile returns. He thinks that it's you and him against the world! Here, the relationship can materialize and grow organically and without the games. When a couple reaches the point of the *Pennies in the Jar* (great memories), they grow and you become an unstoppable force! The more pennies, the stronger you become as a couple.

SECRET #7: The Wrong Guy Will Try to Draw You Back!

I see this all the time. A woman will get everything right, she has a great story behind her, she stays in shape, she is smart, and she screams high-value but the same **wrong** guy, or exact similar type, will draw her back in! Don't be tempted by this.

Your ex, a wet kitten, will try and try again to get you back by promising that "This time it will be different." Then, even when you do dump him, the same wrong guys will keep popping up in your life because you are subconsciously looking for them.

You might have read all my books, too, so you have come to understand men.

But something still stands in your way.

Women tend to choose the same type of guy that rejects them.

I am seeing this more and more. Talking to all my wonderful readers like you gives me an advantage, and I am sure that I am on to something here. I constantly see women comparing a new, quality, guy to an old flame that did not work out. She will say things like, "The attraction is not there." or "I miss the crazy sex with my ex and I don't see this happening with my current guy."

Women (men might too, but I need more proof before I can make a sure statement) stay attracted to the very toxic things that failed them in their past relationship. Sometimes it's the drama of breaking up and making up. Sometimes it's the screaming and the fighting. Sometimes it's the cheating or the bad-boy attitude. This drama, in some warped way, becomes exciting to them and they want more of it. It is comfortable because it is normal. The "new guy" is boring because he simply wants to love without the toxic drama!

What?

Yes I am seeing it, yet many don't even realize it. Fighting has become such the norm that some women feel it is a part of a healthy relationship when it is not. Love comes easy and it is drama free for the most part. Successful couples rarely fight and when they do it is always with respect. Healthy relationships are happy and respectful – you come home knowing exactly where you stand and he has dinner on the table instead of another woman in the bed! Stability is the norm. Both of you act like yourselves all the time.

I have seen women who are shocked by their first healthy relationship. They don't like it because they might not have ever experienced it. But you know what happens after a short period of time? They usually cry with happiness as they start to understand how easy and how wonderful love can be.

I believe women need to try to date different guys, guys that are outside of their comfort zone, and see where it goes.

I had a reader come to me and tell me that she met a new guy and he did everything right. He took her out the old-fashioned way to dinner, she met the family, he was chivalrous, he was self-employed, he waited on sex, and he expressed his interest in being monogamous.

What did she do? She dumped him because she didn't feel the same chemistry as the guy who cheated on her for the better part of three years! It was easy for her because her cheating ex was always there, breathing down her neck, promising change that never came.

Hmmm.

Don't wait until your 65 to realize that your best friend, who was always there for you, who was single and loved you, was the guy you should have dated and married all along.

Don't keep throwing out the guys that will commit and keep choosing the guys that won't.

Expand out. Double down. Date guys you would not date normally. Covet the nice things he does and realize that this is what you want. Sometimes the most obvious things are in plain sight and women (and men) don't even see them. If you can't realize the difference of toxic traits versus loving, healthy, traits then you are too close to your ex.

Be single for a while. Get distance. Get to a place where you can look back and understand the harm your past relationship caused and choose someone different. Drama is not healthy.

SECRET #8: Give a Man "Perceived Freedom"

Let's expand on Secret #4, *Release the Chains*, because I have a new experience to share while writing this book!

I was in South Beach last week and I called my married friend Ted who lives there to see if he wanted to grab a drink. Very few of our mutual friends had heard from Ted and I soon found out why. Ted is married to a very controlling wife (meaning a woman with low confidence and deep trust issues) named Cynthia.

I gave Ted the heads up but he still did not contact me back. I texted him. He finally texted me back and said that Cynthia and he had plans so he couldn't get together and that he was very sorry.

Are you kidding me?

Ted was one of my closest friends and he would **never** blow me off. My other friends confirmed that his wife gave him absolutely zero freedom. They had tried to get him to go golfing many times, and finally gave up.

To me, this is unacceptable. A man needs freedom, or in the least *perceived freedom*. Let me explain.

Let's get back to a man's DNA. Ingredient #6 is *status and how we measure up to our peers rank high,* remember? Ted could not answer the call from me. That means he lost his status with me, and he knows it. He feels emasculated! I don't even have to ask him – I know he does because I know him!

I also know that contempt is building against his wife. He is feeling constricted and restrained and someday soon, he will resist her unless something counters this inevitable outcome. And when I say "resist her" I mean their relationship will be over.

You see, a man needs to feel that he has freedom. He knows that he is happily married, but take away all his friends and immature adventures that he enjoyed so much throughout the previous years, and you kill the man. There must be trust. Guys should be allowed to enjoy a golfing weekend and women should do the same. When my friends are in town, married or single, I should be able to go out with them, assuming I have some notice. I should be encouraged, too! And men should reciprocate this freedom to their significant others, as well.

Do this and you give your man that "perceived freedom" that I talk about. Sure, he knows that he is married and has kids, but he can still go and have some fun with his friends once in a while.

"So Gregg, two weeks in Vegas is cool in your book?"

NO!

There are limits, of course, but when a couple has confidence and trust, a night or weekend getaway, once in a while, is a healthy thing for both of them. It allows them to miss one another. Trust me, after two days of being **stupid** with my friends I want to come home!

Perceived Freedom.

Now you know something that you have never heard before and you can add it (and apply it) to your new list of understanding men items!

SECRET #9: Act like a Guy on Occasion

This Man Mode concept works extremely well and aligns with my narrative towards communicating with men effectively – mirror him. Basically, do what he does **before** he does it to you. If he acts a certain way toward you, then he obviously understands that this is what works best for him and makes him feel most comfortable, right?

So do the same thing to him!

Let's look at a real example.

Last night I got this email from one of my readers:

Hi Gregg,

My boyfriend gives compliments to other women in front of me. I know he loves me a lot. But I do not like it when he compliments other women with such genuine intensity. Example: He said yesterday that he loves how one of my female friends talks; she sounds so innocent and sweet. Is it natural to feel jealous and sad at such comments? Or am I oversensitive about it? I did not say anything to him about it yet. But I was thinking I should address it to him in such a way that he does not feel I am a petty person, I wish he had said that about me. Can you help me figure out what to do here and how to address this problem?

Thanks – Kate

My answer:

> *Hi Kate! Guys can be jerks like that. I would be offended too if this happens often, although what he said was not too bad. Let's take a different tact! Fight fire with fire. Don't whine about this to him, instead, like I always say – do what he does to you, back to him (mirror him) and watch what happens. The next time he says something about a woman, counter with a compliment about a guy. Say something like this:*
>
> *"Talk about a voice, our waiter last night must get any woman he wants with his dreamy voice!"*
>
> *The key is to deliver it like you mean it and don't make it seem like you are just mad and trying to get even. Now he will feel what you feel! If he doesn't, then turn it up a notch. And if he gets mad or comments, say, "You give compliments all the time, why can't I?"*
>
> *– Gregg*

This works great. Suddenly, Kate's boyfriend understands exactly how she feels when he compliments other women. This was a "shot across his bow" suggesting that he wise up. The beauty is that it hits Peter (let's call him) much harder than Kate. Why? **Look at the list above** – Kate just got results by stirring up challenge, competition, and the need to rank superior over other men. He just "lost" in the comparison battle over who has a better voice. Kate's boyfriend probably won't be poking that hornet's nest again.

I will guarantee that Peter will think twice about handing out compliments in front of Kate. But this gets even better. Not only was the problem solved without any bitching or whining, Kate just re-trained her man without him even knowing it **and** she gained his respect!

Acting like a guy works!

So now this simple solution can be plugged into, and solve, so many situations quicker than a groundhog can eat cabbage without any of the contempt.

- *You are arguing and he is about to clam up and head to his man cave.* You clam up first and head to your chick retreat.

- *He is ready to fall asleep after sex.* You kick him out of bed and send him home because you want to sleep.

- *Your boyfriend or husband is spending too much time with his friends.* Encourage him to be with them but make plans ahead of him to be with your girls.

Your partner will be amazed and left scratching his head. He will be asking himself, "What just happened here?" Then he will mumble under his breath, "I love this woman!"

Are these just a bunch of games? Hell yeah they are! But they are effective and fun games that make your point **crystal** clear and shout to him, "I am a high-value woman so you better step up your game, kid!" And the more he knows that you know how to play the game, **the less** it needs to get played. In the examples above, you are simply acting like he acts towards you so he can feel what you feel. When he does, your point is made and he becomes trained to be a good boy!

Sit, Johnny, sit!

Ahhh, the mind of the common man. He is such a simple creature indeed ☺.

SECRET #10: A Man will Say or Do Anything to Keep You Hooked

Sad fact, huh?

Last year I had a guy contact me, laughing, at how long he had kept his girl convinced they were going to get married. He was dating others on the side. He even bought her a ring knowing full well it was just for show.

I blasted him and called him a*****e. Sorry for my language. What I should have done was go along with his ploy, found out who his fiancée was, and turned his ass in. I wish I had.

My secret is that some guys will do anything to string women along because the sex is good and they are very comfortable with how things are.

Now, some men are emotionally unavailable and think (hope, even) that something in their minds will make them commit but they find out they still can't. I understand this – some men are just so wounded they can't have a healthy relationship, but until they realize this they keep trying.

The bad ones will talk about having kids, tell you they have never met a woman quite like you, talk about (but never take) that trip to Italy, blah, blah, blah.

But now that you know this secret, what are you to do?

Keep Your Options Open

Always keep your options of men wide open until one of them steps up and shows you something real! Try to date multiple men so that you maintain these options. If you can't handle this, then keep a large and vibrant social life thriving with activities so you have a quality pool of men to date at any given time. Limited options make a woman choose what's in front of them and these men are often low-hanging fruit.

Set Time Limits

A high-value woman constantly has her "commitment clock" running. If her relationship is moving along comfortably, doing the things I teach in this book, she will be in full control and know what is going on with her man. This man will know that he is **damn lucky** to be with her and if gets out of line and does not meet her reasonable timeline to get married (or whatever her end goal is), she will be gone in a NY minute!

Watch His Actions, Never His Words

This is not foolproof, as witnessed by my story above, but few men can (or will) fake multiple actions suggesting that he is in love. The guy above had lots of money so the ring was no big deal but for many men, they could not take this step nor would they. If a man is spending money and time to be with you, respects you, is protecting you, and socially announcing you, then these are strong signs that he is a good man.

Listen to What Others Say

If a guy meets your family and friends, and you meet his, and everyone agrees that he is a good guy, then chances are (in combination with my others pointers) you are not getting played.

And Finally, Let Your Hair Down!

Show your man every side of your crazy and awesome personality! Test him. Push him. Challenge him. *Get him out of his comfort zone with you.* High-value women do these things because they ooze confidence. There is nothing worse than finding out bad things about a man 10 years later because you were too afraid to push his buttons early on in your life together.

Do these things and you will learn everything about him so you can have the information to make the right decision to stay or go. A quality **Lion** will love these challenges and a wet kitten will pee on the rug, run, and try stalking an easier target – not you!!

CHAPTER 5
A Real Life Example
Showing How Change Can Save a Marriage

Valerie was ready for change. She contacted me with the following story:

Her husband had moved out and left her with their two kids. He still chimed in now and then to visit the kids whenever he felt the need and to have sex with his (now separated) wife. Valerie was crying like crazy. She had no hope of getting him back or moving on. Erik (we will call him) still paid some of the bills (barely) so she could keep the apartment and "exist." Valerie did have a good job (albeit low paying) and she told me that she kept getting offered a promotion but her self-confidence was so beat up that she didn't understand why it had been offered to her, nor did she even want to take the promotion.

The poor woman probably spent her last dime to hire me. We had talked several times by email after she read my books. She told me how he had total control over her, did what he wanted, dated when he felt like it, and constantly put her down.

You see, Valerie was so motivated for change I knew she would do whatever it took to turn her life around – **and that's all I needed to be able to help her!**

I went to work!

I sent her my confidence course, Comfortable in Your Own Shoes. We worked together on affirmations so she could "break her negative thoughts that her husband had instilled in her." We came up with her vision of where she was going to be in 6 months, 1 year, and 5 years from today. Then we formed her road map to get her there starting the next day! She whipped together a vision board showing her new car, her new apartment with a back yard, and a new man (not her ex) in her life … **she was getting excited!**

Valerie still did **not** yet believe any of this could happen, but I told her that she was getting excited because **she was starting to believe!**

Simultaneously, we worked on her ex. She stopped having sex with him! She had her Mom do the switch when it was his turn to take the kids so that Valerie wouldn't have an emotional break down when she saw Erik. I put up a "fire-wall," basically, between all communications and ran inter-ference so Valerie could work on herself. All communication went through me without Erik ever knowing what hit him or that I was even involved.

Valerie worked up the confidence and got the raise that we knew she could get but was too beat down to accept. Her Mom, seeing progress in her daughter, stepped up and lent her a small sum of money and baby sat more often. Her Mom being on board helped Valerie with her self-esteem, too. This also allowed Valerie to have the occasional night to herself! I instructed her to make a goal to meet two new, fun wing-women! She joined a group and met *three* new single moms in somewhat similar positions. They flourished together and supported each other. Because there were now three of them, they could rotate babysitting while the other two went out. This saved everyone money and now Valerie had the power of three!

Valerie then joined a gym and started getting in shape. We found a gym (YMCA) that offered free babysitting, so that worked out perfect.

Her confidence was growing stronger and stronger every day.

Erik, who was pissed off at what was happening in front of his eyes, suddenly started being nice, texting her and asking her what she was up to. He had interest in his wife again. The challenge was back. Erik wanted to come home! Valerie had some decisions to make. Should she take him back? Or should she continue on her wonderful path?

Valerie chose to stay separated for now, and is dating a great guy. She and I have stayed close to this day. We have a laugh when we talk because she now holds **all** the cards – not Erik!

This is what I do! And my eyes tear up when I can "stir the giant from within." Valerie found her giant last year – **you can too!**

The moral of the story?

Just like the previous chapters, I got Valerie to understand Erik's DNA and use it in her favor. Erik was bored. The challenge was gone. Does that make Erik a bad person? You can decide that. I am just telling you that this can happen to any "good" man. You see, we can't necessarily control what drives us (our DNA mix) but you can feed us what we need to steer us in the right direction!

Valerie succeeded in her mission by working on herself and her own personal story. She put herself ahead of others for once. She made a plan and followed it. She became interesting and exciting again, and Erik noticed. We sprinkled in some life coach tactics, like affirmations, and she was well on her way to confidence and a new and happy life.

Was it difficult? Valerie did not think so. In fact, she thought it was fun! The only difficult part was gaining the knowledge to do all of this and that is where a *male dating coach* and a *life coach* (yours truly) make the difference.

FINAL
THOUGHTS

These are the type of emails I get every day from my readers! I bring this up not to blow sunshine up my butt, no, (you already read the book) I say it in an effort to get you to implement what you just read!

Gregg,

Oh my gosh, thank YOU. You may think I'm a bit crazy for this rant but your book opened my eyes to ridiculous behaviour I've been putting up with in ALL my relationships, not just dating. For someone with an MBA and another Master's degree, from Harvard of all places, I've been incredibly stupid. No other word for it. I really, really appreciated your frankness and want to encourage you to please keep it up. Sometimes people need straightforward, no-nonsense truth. Enough of the traditional nonsense. I think we're living in different times and this is definitely your platform, if I may be so bold. Don't allow anyone to discourage you ... you're helping more people than you think and I for one am eternally grateful.

— Cheryl

Don't just sit back and say "interesting;" instead; read this over and over until you can recite the chapters! Fifty percent of my readers will do nothing, and another fifty percent will take action ... the latter will change their lives for the cost of a Starbucks coffee – 250,000 books sold to date says that what I write works! Let me help you!

Thank you for reading,
Gregg

AUTHOR
BIO

As one of Boston's top dating coaches, my books rest prominently atop the dating advice genre. In my role as a life coach, I've been known to be unorthodox (a good thing) and I break a few rules. I assist both men and women and help them understand one another.

I won't bore you with my professional bio. Instead, I will share with you the story of how I became a dating and life coach and what makes me qualified to coach you.

The irony is that I come from an extremely dysfunctional family. I witnessed the marriage of my parents crumble before my eyes at an early age. Flying dishes seemed normal in my household. I came out a bit angry and I have 12 years of failed relationships to show for it.

But I eventually started encountering positive things in my life. I discovered that couple, that elusive, elderly couple holding hands in the park at the ripe old age of eighty. They gave me hope! As a problem solver, I can solve anything (I believed) ... except relationships, damn it!

I couldn't figure out why my folks represented the norm rather than the exception to married life. Fifty-five percent of all couples experience divorce. Why? "What is wrong?" I asked myself.

In 2009, after a long stretch of living the single life, I experienced an epiphany. I attended a Christmas show at my Dad's church. I am not a religious person, but when I saw the cheerful couples and witnessed the powerful music, I was touched. I **needed** answers to love and I **wanted** true love for myself.

I was tired of my shallow life as a single. I decided to study my failures and interview as many single people and couples as I could. I even watched the movie, Hitch, and it motivated me to help others.

I realized that I possessed a natural ability to help others discover love, and discovered it was my future. Can you guess where I started? Yep, those elusive, elderly, happy couples. Sure, I got maced a few times as I approached them with questions, but the knowledge I gained was priceless!

Since then, I've sat down with thousands of people; happy couples, unhappy couples, single people of all types, and everything in between. I quickly learned that confidence played a large role in both attracting and keeping a partner.

My friends encouraged me to launch a dating advice website. I now own the top dating site for women, WhoHolds-TheCardsNow.com. Women (and men) contact me after reading my books. I have become a "Dear Abbey" of sorts. Today, after thousands of interviews, I have accomplished my goal; I broke the code and enjoy a great relationship myself. Now I plan to share my findings with YOU!

I realized, even though people believed what I taught, that they suffered a serious problem. They lacked the motivation and confidence to execute my tactics. A course change was required. I started concentrating on life coaching in addition to relationship coaching. If you can't love yourself, how can you love someone else? It's impossible.

Now, I concentrate on pulling people in and guiding them to understanding themselves. I assist them in creating clarity in their lives, setting goals, and creating the path to attain those goals. I offer inspiration, passion, and spirituality with the constant **live like you're dying** attitude. People are transformed through my books and daily exercises.

I have written 14 Amazon Best Sellers, four of which attained #1 Best Seller status. Together we can build your confidence, increase your self-esteem, and propel you closer to your goals. You will discover happiness by completing the work most people will never attempt!

Today, I travel and teach in all the sexy playgrounds: LA, South Beach, and Las Vegas. I can assist in your journey to build confidence so we can transform your life.

I am not merely a best-selling author, my readers are my friends and I communicate with them directly. I humbly ask you to allow me to assist you. Join me on my quest for your happiness, your exciting journey to an extraordinary life!

Gregg Michaelsen,
Confidence Builder

GET THE WORD OUT TO YOUR FRIENDS!

If you believe your friends would draw something valuable from this book, I'd be honored if you'd share your thoughts with them. If you feel particularly strong about the contributions this book made to your success, I'd be eternally grateful if you would post a review on Amazon. You can check them out by clicking the links below. My men's dating advice books are listed after the women's books.

Women's Dating Advice Books

Please read the jewel of all my books: *To Date a Man, You Must Understand a Man*; this companion book to all my books will help you understand men! Read the hundreds and hundreds of reviews to learn how well my tactics work!

One of my latest books is selling like crazy: *Pennies in the Jar: How to Keep a Man for Life* is the ultimate women's guide to keeping a relationship strong!

More Awesome Best Sellers
to Solve Your Dating Issues!

- Single and looking? Read *The Social Tigress*

- Want to learn about more about men?
  Read *Manimals: Understanding Different Types of Men and How to Date Them*

- Ready for a serious change? Read *Own Your Tomorrow*

- Want to text a man into submission? #1 Best Seller: *Power Texting Men*

- Take yourself on a self-discovery Journey by reading *To Date a Man You Must Understand Yourself*

- Need your ex back? I'll give you your best chance with *How to Get Your Ex Back Fast*

- Want to regain control of your relationship? Try *Who Holds the Cards Now?*

- Confidence attracts! Get it here: *Comfortable in Your Own Shoes*

- Want to clean up Online? Read *Love is in The Mouse* and *Love is in the Mouse 2017*

- Over 40 and getting back into the scene? Check out *Middle Aged and Kickin' It*

- Need some introvert dating help? Take a peek at *Be Quiet and Date Me!*

- And for the long distance couple: *Committed to Love, Separated by Distance*

I can be reached at *Gregg@WhoHoldsTheCardsNow.com*.

Please visit my website just for women:
https://www.whoholdsthecardsnow.com/
Facebook: *WhoHoldsTheCardsNow*
Twitter: *@YouHoldTheCards*
I'm a *Your Tango Expert*

Books for Men and Women that Motivate!
*Live Like You're Dying_*
The Power to Communicate

You are my motivation!
Gregg

Made in the USA
Columbia, SC
11 March 2022